Area 51

Discerning Facts
from Fiction

Conrad Bauer

ISBN: 9798584406547

Printed in the United States

MAPLEWOOD
PUBLISHING

Contents

Hiding in Plain Sight

There have been whispered rumors about a secret base somewhere in the Nevada desert for decades. In its early days, the "Nevada Test Site" was known for the fiery atomic blasts that took place there. Although the nuclear testing program was ostensibly top-secret, it was kind of hard to hide the smoking gun of a mushroom cloud. Back in the late 1940s and early 1950s, in fact, area residents used to hold watch parties where they would sit outside and enjoy the toasty glow of the gamma rays. So much for duck and cover!

During the 1960s and 1970s, it was also generally known that top-secret military aircraft were being tested at the installation near Groom Lake. However, most people had better things to do than venturing into the inhospitable wasteland to get a peek, and the base's existence was little more than a local curiosity.

It wasn't until the 1980s that Area 51 truly entered the national spotlight. In 1984, TV producer Jaime Shandera received an anonymous envelope in the mail. It contained documents purporting to be a highly classified memo describing a secret UFO study group called Majestic 12— and claiming that living extraterrestrials and their spacecraft had been transported to Area 51. Shandera didn't reveal the mysterious documents until 1987. But once he did, it was like a bomb went off.

A year later a major expose on UFOs called *UFO Cover-Up? Live!* appeared on network TV, detailing in part a secretive base in Nevada where alien beings had allegedly been taken. The aliens were supposedly under the care of the U.S. government and from time to time were treated to... strawberry ice cream. Now, the claim that Uncle Sam was hosting extraterrestrial visitors was intriguing; the assertion that he was serving them strawberry ice cream seemed slightly ridiculous. Predictably, it ended up becoming the most memorable part of the program, completely overshadowing the more astonishing material presented— and some have since argued that it might have been a bit of disinformation thrown into the mix to make the rest of the stunning info seem less believable. Then again, reality is usually stranger than fiction, so who really knows? Maybe ETs do like strawberry ice cream after all!

At any rate, a year after this TV show aired a guy named Bob Lazar came forward with his own tale of UFOs and ETs at Area 51. He hadn't seen a gray-skinned alien slurping up strawberry ice cream on the base, but he did claim to have been briefed with documents indicating that the U.S. military was well aware of aliens and their spacecraft. His natural suspicions as to the veracity of those documents had then vanished when he was assigned to work on an alien reactor that could generate gravitational fields.

It was after Lazar told his Area 51 story that Dreamland became a household name. But even though it was clearly visible through high powered telescopes and in satellite imagery, military officials continued to insist that they didn't know anything about it. In the ensuing years, it became kind of a running gag to talk about the base that didn't officially exist—but when former Area 51 employees began dying of cancer in the 1980s and 1990s, it wasn't quite so funny anymore. Several lawsuits prompted an unofficial admission in 1994, and then in 2013, the government finally came clean and admitted what the whole world already knew—yes, Area 51 does exist.

The base may thus have lost some of its mysterious sheen, but it still attracts plenty of interest—as was demonstrated in 2019 when over two million people declared over the internet their desire to "Storm Area 51." In the end, thankfully enough, this would-be assault on a military installation by an army of social media trolls devolved into nothing more than a few drunks wandering around the Nevada desert. But the publicity the nonevent generated serves as a clear demonstration of just how powerful the imagery of Area 51 remains.

This book follows both the known history and the *unknown* history of the world's most secretive facility that's been hiding in plain sight for all of these years.

A Mysterious Military Industrial Complex Takes Root

The rumors and conspiracy theories surrounding Area 51 are so fantastic that the more skeptical among us might once have been tempted to tell ourselves that the entire place was a myth. But even if you don't believe in UFOs, aliens, and reverse-engineered spacecraft, you can now rest assured that Area 51 is very real. Its existence was officially acknowledged in 2013, and it has a history stretching back well over half a century before that.

The military first set up shop in the region back in 1940, when America was already gearing up for World War Two. Looking for a secure and remote location to test out the latest in munitions, the U.S. Army acquired some three million acres of Nevada desert that would later be called the Las Vegas Bombing and Gunnery Range.

The next big development came in the late 1940s when the site was designated by the Atomic Energy Commission for testing of nuclear bombs. The Commission created a numbered grid system to identify specific "Areas" of the site, and Area 51 was initially just another run-of-the-mill section on this grid. Soon, though, the newly created U.S. Air Force moved into a section of Area 51 called Groom Lake, and shortly after that, they partnered with the CIA on something called Project AQUATONE.

By this point in the 1950s, the icy chill of the Cold War had completely frozen U.S. relations with the Soviet Union. The Americans had no idea what their rival nuclear superpower was doing behind the Iron Curtain, and they wanted to find out. Project AQUATONE entailed developing a plane that could out-fly the Soviets and sail unmolested through Soviet airspace while a CIA pilot took pictures of what the Reds were up to down below. Specifically, they needed an aircraft that could fly higher than anything else in the world. What they came up with was the U-2 spy plane. The first U-2 prototype made its maiden flight on August 4, 1955. With a flight ceiling of 70,000 feet, the U-2 was truly revolutionary. It could fly far higher than Soviet planes of the era, and it was even difficult for Soviet ground radar to track.

Nevertheless, the Americans weren't taking any chances. The last thing they needed was the Soviets shooting down a U.S. Air Force plane and using it as an excuse to start World War Three. It was for this reason that they used only CIA agents, rather than Air Force officers, as pilots for the U-2. Instead of USAF insignia, they slapped NACA logos on the plane's sides. NACA, the National Advisory Committee for Aeronautics, was the direct predecessor of NASA, and in the event that a U-2 pilot had to bail out over enemy territory, it was hoped that he could avoid being shot as a spy by claiming that he was a civilian monitoring meteorological phenomena and had simply been blown off course. Many of the CIA pilots, though, were skeptical that the Russians would go for such a yarn—so much so, that it was standard procedure to bring a cyanide capsule along for the flight.

After five years of flying the U-2, the CIA's luck finally ran out when a pilot named Gary Powers was shot down by a Soviet

SAM (surface-to-air missile) in the spring of 1960. Newspapers erupted with headlines about how the Russians had shot down a "spy plane" and the U.S. was forced to reveal the U-2 to the world. Interestingly enough, when Powers was being interrogated by the Russians, one of the questions they kept asking him repeatedly was about Area 51. Yes, long before the American public knew much of anything about the secretive base, the KGB had already picked up on it. But the existence of Area 51 was one secret that Gary Powers was not willing to give up, and no matter how much the Soviets grilled him about the home base of his unusual aircraft, he lied and told them it was in California.

Powers was ultimately released in 1962 when the Russians agreed to exchange him for a spy of theirs whom the Americans had been holding. Meanwhile, the unexpected shoot-down of his U-2 had sent the folks at Area 51 literally back to the drawing board.

Where History and Legend Begin to Converge

What we have seen so far in this book is the known history of Area 51. But when it comes to Area 51, just a little off the beaten track of the known history lies the shadowy and much more uncertain trail of *unknown* history. According to some conspiracy theorists, this unknown history began back in the 1950s while the CIA was still tinkering with the first U-2 spy planes.

The story comes from an anonymous source who was interviewed by Ufologist Richard Dolan in 2013. President Dwight Eisenhower, who had just recently been sworn into office, had apparently heard rumors that the U.S. Army had recovered a flying disk—in other words, a UFO—and that it was being tested out at Groom Lake. Concerned that a military-industrial complex of epic proportions had begun to run amok at Area 51, Ike wanted to know what in the Sam Hill was going on.

He allegedly sent some of his aides out to Area 51 to find out—and Dolan's source, who related all of this information just prior to his passing, claimed to have been one of them. The whistle-blower was an agent in the fledgling CIA, and he and his boss were personally shouted at by Eisenhower, who declared, "I want you and your boss to fly out there, I want you to give them a personal message, and tell whoever is in charge, tell them that they have a week—this coming week— to get to Washington, and to report to me, and if they don't,

I'm gonna get the First Army of Colorado and we're going to go over and take the base over. I don't care what kind of classified material you got; we're going to rip this thing apart!"

The threat from this former five-star general to literally send in the troops must have gotten the attention of the Area 51 brass. When Ike's team arrived at the facility, they did nothing to stop them from snooping around—in fact, they gave them the grand tour. It started with S4, one of the most secret sections of the secret base—and the same place where infamous Area 51 whistle-blower Bob Lazar would later work. Here the group was shown hangar after hangar filled with off-world vehicles of apparently extraterrestrial design. The operative and his associates were actually allowed to reach out and touch one of the vehicles, and to their astonishment, they were able to push the huge craft as if it were nothing more than a piece of furniture. They would later be informed that this interstellar spacecraft weighed only 150 pounds— quite an improvement on the U-2's eight *tons*! Still, the spacecraft wasn't nearly as startling as the "alien interview" in which the whistle-blower supposedly witnessed a living ET being interrogated by military personnel.

When the agents returned to Washington and made their report to the President, Eisenhower was stunned. Suddenly seeing the point of all that secrecy, he immediately moved to make keeping Area 51 under wraps a top priority. And, of course, he couldn't resist setting up a meeting so that he could see the aliens for himself.

And while the idea of a sitting U.S. president meeting with ET might seem plenty weird enough, things get even weirder. Because according to the really hardcore conspiracy theorists, Ike not only met with the aliens; he made a deal with the aliens. This pact supposedly allowed them to abduct and study a few human beings in exchange for their help in advancing human (or at least U.S. military) technology.

The aliens promised that those they abduct would not be harmed, and would be returned with their memories of the experience wiped clean. This is allegedly the source of the abductee phenomenon known as "missing time," in which abductees realize that there are whole hours that they cannot remember or account for. The aliens also agreed to furnish the U.S. government with a list of all their abductees; since they could apparently do a quick scan of someone's brain and know every detail about that person's life, compiling such a list wouldn't be all that difficult for them.

Colonel Philip Corso, another death-bed whistle-blower, seems to corroborate this story in his book *The Day After Roswell*. According to Corso, Eisenhower felt he didn't have much choice but to cooperate with the ETs. He hoped that the promised technological aid would give U.S. scientists enough of a head start to gain some measure of military parity with the aliens, in case they became hostile. Dolan's whistle-blower told a very similar tale, and although he elected to remain anonymous, he can be heard on tape giving this testimony directly to Ufologist Richard Dolan. The man was suffering from a terminal illness and passed away shortly after the recording was made. He supposedly decided to come clean because he knew that he was going to die. Was he telling the truth? No one can be certain—but the time period of which he speaks, the mid-1950s, is the point where the known history of Area 51 and the unknown territory of conspiracies and legends begin to merge.

By the 1970s, according to yet another supposed whistle-blower interviewed by paranormal author / UFO researcher Nick Redfern, the metamorphosis of Area 51 from a secret test facility to an outright dreamland of UFO technology was complete. This source said that the U.S. government's hoard of alien tech was initially spread across the country in places such as Wright–Patterson Air Force Base in Ohio, several installations in Utah, and various others. Sometime in the 1960s, though, it was decided to transfer all things ET to one highly secure facility—and that facility was Area 51.

There is at least one other source who concurs with this, and he is not anonymous. His name is Charles Hall, and he claims that he was hired on as a nuclear physicist at Area 51 in 1964. He believed that he would be doing some very interesting work there, but he was hardly prepared to have his entire understanding of not only physics—but *reality itself*—turned on its head.

Hall says he saw Area 51 personnel interacting with aliens which he refers to as "tall whites" because they were about 8 feet tall and had snow-white, almost glowing skin. The way they let off such an unearthly shimmer, the beings actually reminded him of depictions of angels. He's not saying that they *were* angels; they just reminded him of them—because, besides their unusual height and radiant skin, these entities had human-looking features. Human mouth, eyes, nose, ears, and the like—but even so, as soon as Hall saw these entities, he intuitively knew that they were not of this world. And that was about the *only* thing he knew; as he puts it, "It's such a shock, you are not sure if you are looking at a ghost or an angel, or if you are dreaming."

But as Hall became acquainted with the ETs and their culture, he realized that they were in fact highly intelligent creatures who had developed spacecraft that were able to travel faster than the speed of light. Being a physicist, Hall knew full well what this meant—it meant that Einstein's special theory of relativity was wrong. Einstein had said that nothing could go faster than the speed of light—yet here these beings were, apparently capable of breaking the light barrier at will.

Along with the tall whites, Hall also saw plenty of the classic "gray aliens" that so many Americans claim to have encountered. These most commonly referenced ETs are three to four feet in height, with large heads, large, almond-shaped, all-black eyes, only nostrils where their noses should be, and tiny slits for mouths. And the most famous gray alien to have ever graced Area 51 is a being referred to in UFO lore as J-Rod.

J-Rod was supposedly a 200-year-old alien who in 1953 survived a crash in Kingman, Arizona, just south of Grand Canyon National Park. After J-Rod and the wreckage of his craft were retrieved by the U.S. military, he became a ward of Area 51. But this ET wasn't just a freeloader; he became a helpful member of the team, working alongside human scientists.
Incredible as this sounds, a guy named Bill Uhouse says it really happened. And he should know, because, during the 1950s and 1960s, J-Rod was his supervisor at Area 51! I told you we were going down the rabbit hole, and this one is about as odd as it gets. Nevertheless, Uhouse maintained until the day he died in 2009 that J-Rod advised him and others on replicating the processes of recovered alien

spacecraft—which, even with the alien's help, was still pretty difficult. Uhouse was never quite sure whether his ET coworker was a prisoner, a guest, or an employee—but it seems clear that J-Rod had worked out some kind of agreement with the U.S. military to help its human scientists.

Later reports from an individual who called himself Kewper corroborated some of Bill Uhouse's account. This mysterious individual asserted that he was a language expert who was sent to Area 51 to learn to communicate with J-Rod. This was in the summer of 1958, about the same time Eisenhower sent his underlings to investigate what was happening at Area 51, so it would seem that J-Rod was the being that the team saw that day—and this would mean that J-Rod was encountered by all three of these supposed whistle-blowers. But that's not all. Because in the 1990s, yet another figure came forth to say that he had also had interactions with an alien called J-Rod at Area 51.

This guy, Dan Burisch, claims that he was hired on as a microbiologist and tasked with taking tissue samples from the alien. This was certainly not what he'd expected to be doing when he was hired, but his shock soon gave way to wonder. He was amazed to see this entity living and working with human beings. Despite the constraints of the base, the alien scientist was apparently fairly content. He passed the days in his own personally stabilized environment, which Burisch described as "a perfectly round sphere chamber." Burisch claims that he became a "close friend" of the alien, which led J-Rod to confide in him that "his race had actually inhabited Earth many thousands of years prior, before being forced to leave" due to a series of cataclysmic natural disasters.

14

Such a suggestion is rather intriguing since we know so little about Earth's past. The planet is about four-and-a-half billion years old, yet as far as we know, human beings have only been in existence for some 200,000 years. That means that there are whole unknown epochs of Earth's past in which sentient extraterrestrials could have visited and even colonized the planet, long before humanity even existed—and due to millions or even billions of years of natural erosion, all trace of these ET colonizers would be long gone.

J-Rod told Burisch that after this evacuation of ancient Earth, the aliens had used their advanced technology to "wander the stars" indefinitely. But now that they had drifted back to their old port of call, they had become interested in the current residents. In particular, they were interested in a so-called "lost genetic factor" which human beings have. J-Rod went on to explain that he and his alien brethren also wished to "establish a friendship" with humanity—"if possible."

Yes, such things sound highly intriguing, but whether there is any truth in any of them remains to be seen. Area 51 is a place where history and legend converge, and at times, it's nearly impossible to tell the difference between the two.

An Archangel, a Blackbird, and a Hopeless Diamond

As fascinating (and mind-boggling) as all the tales of alien tech and ET interaction at Area 51 can be, there is no real way to confirm them. As of yet, they remain simply unproven allegations. What we *can* confirm, however, are some of the technological results of the heavy labors that have taken place in Area 51. Whether they were built solely by human hands or with a little help from some extraterrestrial friends is anyone's guess, but Area 51 has produced some rather extraordinary aircraft. Even looking at just what has been declassified, the rundown is quite impressive.

After the high-flying U-2 spy plane was de-emphasized in the 1960s, the U.S. began to look toward even more advanced crafts for both reconnaissance and potential engagement with adversaries. The result was a series of advanced fighters called the Archangels. (The engineers at Area 51 had always referred to the U-2 as the Angel, so it only made sense that its successor craft, designed to surpass it, would be called the Archangel.) Under a high level of security, aircraft developer Lockheed, which had built the U-2, began work on what would become the "fastest air-breathing" aircraft in the world. The Archangel would not only be able to ascend to the edge of the atmosphere like the U-2; it would also be able to take evasive action and (hopefully) out-fly any SAMs the Russians lobbed at it. A dozen Archangel prototypes were created, designated A-1 to A-12, and it was the A-12 that proved the most successful. It had a sleek, swept-back design and was equipped with powerful Pratt and Whitney turbojet engines mid-wing. The A-12 became operational in 1962 and flew for a couple of years before being phased in favor of an even more impressive aircraft based on the Archangel design: the SR-71 Blackbird.

This plane, which debuted in 1964, still holds several flight records to this day. It could fly as high as 90,000 feet, seamlessly sailing through the upper reaches of Earth's atmosphere. At such heights, the pilots of the Blackbird became more like astronauts, forced to wear pressurized suits both for oxygen and to maintain proper bodily function. But impressive as the Blackbird was, it was also expensive, and after a certain Richard Milhouse Nixon became President of the United States in 1969, he began to criticize the program as being too costly for the American budget. Production of the Blackbird was immediately scaled back— but an even more exciting project was in the works.

For it was during the 1970s that engineers at Area 51 really began to pour their know-how into stealth technology. The efforts were being led by Lockheed Martin with a craft they called their "hopeless diamond." Half of the reason behind this pessimistic-sounding name was that a diamond shape would help render the aircraft invisible to radar. The other half was that diamonds just aren't very aerodynamic! Getting an unwieldy diamond-shaped plane into the air was a major challenge, but the engineers at Area 51 soon proved that it wasn't hopeless after all. They found ingenious ways around the problems in aerodynamics presented by a diamond shape, and the first successful stealth fighter flew in 1976 under the name *Have Blue*. This developed into the F-117 Stealth Fighter, whose production began at Area 51 in

November of 1978. The completed craft first flew out of Groom Lake in 1981, under the utmost secrecy. In fact, it was so secret—and its design so radically different—that anyone who saw it flying overhead would have been well justified in calling it a UFO.

The veil was lifted eight years later when the F-117 was introduced to the public in 1988—which interestingly enough was right around the time that a guy named Bob Lazar came forward with some incredible revelations of his own. According to him, the unveiling of stealth technology was just the very tip of the massive iceberg of submerged secrets at Area 51.

Bob Lazar—The Ultimate Area 51 Whistle-blower?

Before he ever set foot in Area 51 in late 1988, Bob Lazar had already established himself as a valuable technician at nearby Los Alamos National Laboratory. Although Los Alamos later tried to deny that Lazar had ever been employed there, an investigative journalist named George Knapp proved that he had when he got his hands on an official phone book (remember those?) for personnel who worked at the lab that year. Lo and behold, Bob Lazar was listed as an employee. Confronted with this evidence, Los Alamos finally admitted that yes, Lazar may have worked *at* the facility, but he hadn't worked *for* it: he had actually worked for an outside contractor named Kirk-Meyer. They also sought to portray Lazar as a lowly grunt, hinting that he might even have been nothing more than a janitor.

Being able to verify Lazar's self-proclaimed status as a physicist would do much to lend credibility to his claims—but it's impossible. According to Lazar, shortly after he blew the whistle on Area 51, the military wiped away all of his educational records. Yes, they deleted his Ph.D., his Master's, his Bachelor's—you name it—in the blink of an eye, so that he would no longer be able to work, and more importantly, would no longer be taken seriously. Who's going to believe a guy who says he's a physicist when he doesn't even have a degree, right?

But there is a chink in that argument because a few years before Lazar came forward, he was showcased in a tech magazine that ran an article clearly identifying him as a physicist who worked at the Los Alamos National Laboratory. And then there's the simple fact that he has maintained his story all of these years. Even in 1990, when he had some legal trouble and was hauled into court, he didn't change his tune. Now if someone is being questioned under oath, you wouldn't expect him to maintain a bogus story like that, would you? He'd probably think about the penalties for perjury, crack under the pressure, and just tell the truth. Well, unless Lazar is one of the most deluded or devious liars in the world, he must have been telling the truth all along. Because no matter what's at stake, he has continued to maintain that he was a physicist who worked at Los Alamos!

He says he was first called over to Area 51 in 1988 and was given a strenuous entrance interview and an exceptionally thorough background check. He first had to get a "Q clearance"—a standard high-level military intelligence clearance—and then something he referred to as "Majestic 22 level clearance." According to Lazar, Majestic is the next level beyond Q—and Majestic 22 is apparently 21 levels higher than that!

It was a lot to go through for a new job, and he hadn't even had the medical screening yet. When he finally attained the proper clearance and was admitted to Area 51, he was immediately led to a private room where a nurse examined his vitals and asked him whether he had any allergies. She then took a "small device that resembled a pushpin" and placed it on a grid that she drew onto Lazar's arm. She told him that she was depositing trace amounts of various chemicals on his skin to make sure he didn't have an adverse reaction. When Lazar asked her what kind of allergens she was testing for, she replied, "I'd like to tell you, but I can't. I really don't know. All I was told is that you, and a lot of other people here, will be working with exotic materials."

In a top-secret complex such as Area 51, it does make sense that all information would be compartmentalized. Everyone involved would know only just enough to get their particular job done, and this nurse was most likely telling the truth when she said she didn't even know what kind of chemicals she was placing on Lazar's skin—let alone anything about little gray men and flying saucers.

As a physicist, on the other hand, Lazar would have to know substantially more. After the nurse cleared him, the handler who had escorted him to the base, a military guy named Dennis, reappeared and led him down a corridor to another private room. Inside was a desk with a massive pile of "blue file folders" stacked up on top. Dennis told Lazar to sit at the desk, and motioning toward the files, advised, "It's important that we get you caught up as quickly as possible about where we've been and the direction the project is going in. Given your present clearance level, these briefings should give you the background information you need. Obviously, this is all confidential information. Once your clearance is upgraded, you'll learn more. I have a number of other tasks to attend to. Do your reading here, and when I'm done with those other matters, I'll come and get you. Any questions? Good. I'll be back."

After Dennis left, Lazar opened up the top file, which was marked as "Overview" material, and found himself on the ground floor of a whole treasure trove of strange and mysterious data. The files described something called Project Galileo, which was apparently a covert military operation to reverse engineer extraterrestrial spacecraft. Lazar's jaw dropped when he read that, but after thinking about it a bit, he remembered that military phraseology can sometimes be so precise as to be almost misleading. The word "extraterrestrial" didn't necessarily mean an alien civilization; it could just refer to a human vessel that had been in space. Perhaps some rogue nation had launched a spacecraft, the U.S. had obtained it, and the folks at Area 51 were now trying to take it apart.

It was a fine theory, but as Lazar kept reading, it fell completely apart. The subsequent files specifically mentioned extraterrestrial entities and craft not of this Earth. Still, Lazar was not quite ready to accept that Area 51 really had its hands on ET tech. His next thought was that this was some sort of test. Maybe he had been handed a pile of misinformation just to test his reaction. Would he flip out? Would he lose his nerve? Or perhaps his handlers just wanted to see if he could keep a secret. There weren't really any aliens or alien tech at Area 51. This was all just a ruse. They were simply feeding him a fantastic tale to see if he would repeat it outside the base.

At any rate, Dennis still wasn't back, so Lazar continued to read the astounding narrative that was presented in the Area 51 files. The documents revealed that a group of aliens from a distant star system had been clandestinely interacting with human beings for about 10,000 years. Since the late 1940s, the U.S. military had acquired several downed alien spacecraft and even a handful of aliens. There were detailed

24

descriptions of the spacecraft, their propulsion systems, and also the biological components of the aliens themselves. There were even pictures of alien autopsies.

But surely this wasn't true, Lazar thought. Surely it was just some kind of test. There were probably people in another room watching him on a hidden camera. These were the sorts of scenarios that ran through Lazar's mind until, after what seemed like centuries, Dennis finally returned and curtly informed the stunned physicist that they were done for the day. Lazar was then led out of the facility and put on a plane to go home. He could barely sleep that night, wondering just what he had gotten himself into.

Nevertheless, the next morning Lazar got out of bed and began his first day as a regular employee at Area 51. He was promptly taken to his work station and partnered with one Barry Castillo. (As you might imagine, a lot of folks on the internet have googled that name, but so far this person has not been definitively identified.) After introducing themselves, the pair got to work right away.

Castillo didn't so much explain what they would be doing as to demonstrate it. He first directed Lazar's attention to two unusual devices. One was a trash-can-sized cylinder that Castillo called an emitter. The other was a half-sphere, about the size of a basketball, which he identified as a reactor. This reactor was sitting atop a small tower on Castillo's desk. Without warning, Castillo pushed the reactor closer to the emitter as he announced, "Watch this!" He then stepped in between the two objects and extended his arm as if he were going to "shake hands," only to have his arm quickly jerk back in the middle of the gesture. Castillo howled in

25

excitement, as if something amazing had just happened, but Lazar didn't get it. From his perspective, it looked like Castillo had simply extended his hand and then pulled it back. What was the big deal? Lazar was about to find out.

Castillo next had Lazar try the same thing himself. Lazar positioned himself exactly where Castillo had and extended his hand. To his amazement, his hand shot backward of its own accord. It was as if some unseen force had pushed him back, like the reverse polarity of a magnet. Lazar was shocked—but Barry Castillo had an even more impressive visual demonstration lined up.

Taking a golf ball, he tossed it between the two devices. As he watched, Lazar saw the ball "arc" through the air toward the objects, but as soon as it got near, it appeared to collide with an unseen force and bounce off of thin air. It shot up into the ceiling, hitting the panel with such force that it broke and sending debris showering down below.

Castillo then began exclaiming excitedly about how the device could produce its own gravitational field. Seriously? Gravity? A device that could harness one of the most powerful forces of nature? Bob Lazar was impressed—and he was beginning to realize that whatever these things were, they hadn't been created by human beings. This stuff was far beyond the current technical capacity of mankind. The demonstration of these otherworldly devices finally forced him to accept that what he had read in those files was not misinformation after all—it was the truth.

Lazar and Castillo's task was to figure out how the alien tech worked. Given that the technology was obviously thousands, if not millions, of years more advanced than anything we Earthlings have, that was no small order. Many of the military's top scientists had tried, and yet this nut was not any closer to being cracked. These were crafts that had made their way between the stars. How had they done it?

As Lazar examined the second level of one of the spaceships, he understood. A reactor such as Castillo had shown him was installed in the craft. This device worked as a gravity amplifier and could essentially warp space and time, bringing faraway destinations up close and personal. Eventually, he figured out that this gravity-amplifying antimatter reactor ran on some strange fuel called "Element 115." This element could not be adequately produced on Earth because the isotopes decayed too rapidly, but where it originated—the double star system of Zeta Reticuli—it was heavy enough to occur naturally.

Lazar and Castillo thus had to find a way to reproduce this substance. As they struggled to figure it out, they mentioned to their handler, Dennis, that they would have a much better understanding of the functionality of the reactor if they could see it inside a working spacecraft. A few days later, they came to the lab to find Dennis there waiting for them. Dennis said that he had gotten permission for them to see an operational spacecraft. He led them out to a hangar that to Lazar's amazement contained an intact flying saucer.

Unlike a conventional aircraft, this vessel had no landing gear; instead, it was just sitting on its belly right on the concrete. It was about 50 feet in diameter and 20 feet tall. The strangest thing was that it was completely seamless:

there were no visible nuts and bolts holding it together. It looked almost as if it had been molded in one piece.

When Lazar and Castillo went inside, they found that it had three levels. The lowest level, in the belly, was apparently the cockpit. It contained three seats that looked like flower petals, and Lazar was surprised by the absence of restraints on these seats. Considering the G-forces of space flight, he figured there would be some sort of harness such as American astronauts wore when rocketing out of Earth's atmosphere. But these ETs did not appear to need any seat belts.

Nor, apparently, did they need anything so gauche as a user interface. There was no sign of any controls, dials, or switches of any sort in the cockpit or anywhere else in the craft. Unlike Star Trek-style spaceships that have a control panel in every corner of the bridge, this vessel just had a solid floor, ceiling, and walls surrounding these three seats. How did they steer this thing? Apparently, in some fashion quite—for lack of a better word—*alien* to human understanding.

On the second level, Lazar and Castillo located the reactor— the same solid cylinder that they had been working on day in and day out. This was the massive power source that allowed the ship to traverse the cosmos, and they would soon see it in action for themselves. After they finished their shipboard tour, Dennis took them back to the first craft they had looked at. This time all of the hangars were open, and Lazar could see eight saucer-type craft in each hangar. Dennis informed them that a "low-performance test" was about to take place, and the saucers began to take off. Lazar noticed that there was a loud hiss before they rose up from the ground, and he could see the "blue glow" of a corona discharge. The craft then became completely silent as they rose smoothly and then "hung in the air" as if fixed in place. They hovered thus for a few minutes before landing with a slight wobble. Dennis then turned to Lazar and Castillo and told them rather unceremoniously, "That's it—now it's time for you guys to get back to work."

But fascinating as this demonstration had been, the two were still at a loss as to how the reactor and emitter produced the effects they had seen. And Bob Lazar, feeling the pressure, began to grow lax with regard to secrecy. He knew that he was under surveillance, but the imposed silence was killing him. He felt too isolated, and so he did something he was never supposed to do—he began to talk.

First, he just told a few friends about what was happening, but as his paranoia began to build, he came to believe that the more people he told, the more insurance he had in case government agents decided that he was expendable—in case, as he put it, he turned up somewhere in the Nevada desert "with a bullet in his head."

Lazar's handlers, meanwhile, were also growing suspicious. They increased their surveillance and began listening in on his phone calls—and they were alarmed to hear a message he left on his friend's answering machine in which he declared, "Hey Goof-on! This is Boof-on! I have the baby pictures for you! I know you need them as soon as possible."

Now, this was actually an inside joke between Lazar and his buddy. In a previous conversation, his friend had mentioned something about MUFON, the Mutual UFO Network where people report UFO sightings. Bob Lazar had joked that he should call himself Boof-on, and his friend Gene would be called Goof-on. Goof-on and Boof-on. It had become kind of a running gag between them. As for the baby pictures? Gene's wife had just had a baby, and Lazar had snapped some photos that he wanted to share.

But the cryptic message set off alarm bells in those who were listening in. They leaped to the conclusion that Lazar was using some sort of code and the "baby pictures" were actually pictures of UFOs. About 45 minutes later, a car pulled into Lazar's driveway. He heard the car's doors slam, quickly followed by someone pounding on his own door. The men he opened it to, identified themselves as government agents and escorted him to his kitchen table, where they sat him down and interrogated him about Goof-on, Boof-on, and the baby pictures. Lazar explained that it was just a joke— Goof-on was a friend of his named Gene, Boof-on was himself, and the baby pictures were pictures of an actual baby—but the gruff interrogators still weren't happy. They made him sign a piece of paper in which he identified Gene's full name, writing in parentheses (AKA Goof-on).

Their visit left Lazar in the strange place of being slightly amused yet frightened at the same time. He felt so alone, and he wanted to let people know what was happening to him. So he started taking some of his friends out to the outskirts of Area 51 late at night, where they would sit outside of their cars and watch test flights in the distance. When they got lucky, they would see a bright light rising, making stunning "staircase" maneuvers. The light would be, say, 500 feet in the air, and then in the blink of an eye, it would suddenly climb to 1500 feet. It moved so fast that you didn't see it accelerating. It was on one step of the staircase, and then it was suddenly several steps higher—in an instant. This was clearly no ordinary aircraft.

Lazar was glad to be able to share his experiences with others, but he knew that he was jeopardizing his career and quite possibly his life. This was confirmed when Dennis showed up at his home, ordered Lazar into his car, and told him to drive him to the Indian Springs Air Force Base. Lazar was surprised because he thought the base was abandoned. As they drove, he began wondering if this would be the end of the line for him. Was this base going to be his burial ground?

When they got there, though, the base wasn't abandoned after all. Lazar was taken through the gates and escorted into an office. An angry Dennis sat down in front of him, got right in his face, and demanded, "When we told you this was a highly classified project, what made you think you could tell your friends about it? Do you not understand the nature of the agreements you signed? Are you not aware of the consequences of violating those agreements? What were you doing out there—and why were you there with those people?"

Lazar tried his best to downplay his nighttime excursions, claiming that he had just wanted to take his friends out to see some of the action from a distance. He assured Dennis that he hadn't given them any classified information; he'd just wanted them to see some of the test flights, which anybody could do as long as they kept out of the restricted area.

Dennis didn't buy it. Becoming so serious it was scary, he told Lazar, "Don't you know that this project is more important than any of us? More important than your life. More important than mine."

Lazar protested, "They just thought they were lights in the sky. It's not like I told them that these were saucers that aliens were flying."

Dennis didn't seem to like this statement at all. Had Lazar inadvertently given voice to a hidden reality at the base? Although he had never seen who—or what—was operating the saucers during the flight demonstration, he had been inside them and noted that they were not outfitted for a fully grown human. Could it be that ETs were test flying the saucers under orders of the U.S. military? Was that J-Rod up there?

Whatever the truth was, Dennis grew highly agitated at the suggestion. He ordered the other personnel to leave the room and then brought forth a form and ordered Lazar to write down the names and contact information of all of the people he had brought out to view the test flights. Lazar complied, although he tried to keep everything as vague as possible in order to avoid jeopardizing his friends.

After Dennis abruptly announced, "We're done here," Lazar was escorted home. But he knew that it wasn't over. He knew that Area 51 would hound him for the rest of his life. And as the pressure of the surveillance continued to build, he decided that he had to do something. The only way out of the trap he was in was to go public with all he knew. It was then that he contacted Las Vegas journalist George Knapp and broke the story to the world.

Needless to say, Lazar's days of working at Area 51 were done. What remains to be seen is whether or not Barry Castillo or anyone else was ever successful in cracking open the secrets of that alien reactor.

Area-51's Plausible Deniability of Majestic 12

If there's one thing that's not particularly secret about Area 51, it's that it's a military installation. So it might seem like a no-brainer that whatever is going on there, the U.S. military is in charge of it. But when you look back at the history of the base and its heavy CIA involvement, you find at least one instance of overlap in authority. And when you look at some of the wilder conspiracy theories, you find everyone from the Illuminati to the ETs themselves running the place.

But probably the greatest secret society mythos attached to Area 51 is that of the Majestic 12. You'll remember that Bob Lazar says he needed a "Majestic" security clearance to work at the base, and while he never makes any overt mention of the supposed secret panel of experts called the Majestic 12, the congruence is thought-provoking.

The Majestic 12 supposedly began as a kind of UFO study group created by President Harry S. Truman in the wake of the 1947 Roswell Crash. MJ-12, as it is often called, was an elite group of specialists tasked with getting to the bottom of the alien/UFO enigma. Truman's point man in the Majestic 12 was supposedly his Secretary of Defense, James Forrestal. The 11 other members of the group included military men such as General Hoyt Vandenberg, Major General Robert Montague, General Nathan F. Twining, Rear Admiral Roscoe Hillenkoetter, Rear Admiral Sidney Souers, and Gordan Gray, who was an Assistant Secretary of the Army. The rest were technical and scientific advisers: Dr. Vannevar Bush, Dr. Detlev Bronk, Dr. Lloyd Berkener, Dr. Jerome Hunsaker, and Dr. Donald Menzel.

These were all high-profile men holding high-level security clearances—with the one exception of Dr. Donald Menzel. Dr. Menzel was a writer, an academic, and a well-known UFO skeptic who had written several books and reports which ridiculed and debunked the UFO phenomenon. It's perplexing that someone so close-minded about UFOs would be part of an ultra-secret UFO task force, and even more perplexing that as far as anyone knew, Dr. Menzel never had a high-level security clearance.

In 1986, however, UFO researcher Stanton Friedman made an astonishing discovery when he talked to Dr. Menzel's widow. She gave Friedman access to her late husband's "archives at Harvard," and after a bit of searching, he found evidence that not all was as it seemed with Dr. Menzel. Friedman purportedly "discovered that Menzel had Top Secret Ultra clearance from the CIA and had a thirty-year association with the NSA."

If this is true, why would the government secretly employ a man to investigate UFOs and then turn around and unleash him on the public to attack them? Well, it wouldn't have been the only time this has happened. Just take a look at the well-known life of Project Blue Book's J. Allen Hynek. Project Blue Book was the Air Force's public investigation of the UFO phenomenon that ran until 1969, with Dr. Hynek as a top scientist. Initially, Dr. Hynek was famous for being a skeptic and steadfastly debunking any and all alleged UFO sightings. Under his steely gaze, every extraordinary encounter was reduced to nothing more than the moon, the planet Venus, or even more insultingly—swamp gas. Yet, for some reason, when Project Blue Book was shut down, Dr. Hynek had a last-minute conversion and went from being the ultimate skeptic to becoming a true believer. It remains unclear just what his motivations were, but it goes to show that someone could potentially position themselves as a skeptic when they actually believe the phenomenon is real. Take this a step further and you have Dr. Menzel, who allegedly knew it was real yet publicly denounced UFOs as utter rubbish.

The Majestic 12 documents first surfaced on December 11, 1984, when a TV producer named Jaime Shandera received a nondescript package with a manila envelope inside. The envelope contained a canister of microfilm with images of old, timeworn documents that described how President Truman had put together a panel of experts—the Majestic 12—to look into the UFO phenomenon that had come to prominence in the late 1940s. This group of experts supposedly not only concluded that UFOs were of extraterritorial origin but even got their hands on crashed spacecraft and alien beings that had been stored at Ohio's

Wright–Patterson Air Force Base before being sent off to the most secure facility the world had ever known—Area 51—sometime in the early 1950s.

It was at this point that President Eisenhower succeeded President Truman, and as mentioned earlier, Ike soon realized that something highly classified was going on at Area 51 and demanded to be let in on the secret. Going even further into the world of conspiracy, it's alleged that shortly after Eisenhower was debriefed and welcomed into the inner circle of Majestic 12, a meeting was arranged and a deal was struck between the ETs and the United States.

The envelope which contained the Majestic 12 documents had been postmarked in Albuquerque, New Mexico, but it had no return address and proved impossible to trace. Why it had been sent to Shandera was a little easier to figure out; Shandera was at the time actively collaborating with UFO researcher Bill Moore on an investigation into the Roswell Crash and the alleged cover-up that followed. And you have to give Moore and Shandera a whole lot of credit for the patience they displayed in their investigation. Instead of going public with the documents as soon as they showed up, they spent the next three years quietly confirming their authenticity. It wasn't until 1987 that they finally revealed the contents of the MJ-12 papers to the world.

The UFO community—as is often the case—was split right down the middle when it came to the documents. Some researchers, such as the late great Stanton Friedman, were completely convinced that they were the real deal. Others felt that they were probably some sort of misinformation at best, or maybe even an outright hoax. One of their major criticisms is that Truman's signature on the MJ-12 papers appears to be identical to that on a memo that Truman had written to Vannevar Bush in October of 1947. Handwriting experts will tell you that no two signatures are ever exactly identical, so it would seem that there are some problems with the MJ-12 document. Was Truman's signature simply copy-pasted from another historical source to lend the material an aura of authenticity?

Yet if the MJ-12 papers were a complete hoax, you would think that after 30 some years, the hoaxer would have admitted it by now. And as of this writing, no hoaxer has come forward. That's why many others have considered that the documents might have been part of a disinformation campaign aimed at distracting the public from top-secret military projects and—in the oft-repeated phrase—what's was really going on at Area 51.

It is true that the U.S. Air Force has used UFO mythology as a smokescreen for their own top-secret aircraft. They were more than happy to let folks believe that when they saw something shiny and silver reflecting the sun high up in the sky, it was a UFO, not a spy plane. On the other hand, allowing the public to assume that secret aircraft are UFOs is one thing; crafting a whole stack of fake documents discussing UFOs and aliens at great length is another.

For some, this has led to a third possible scenario called "plausible deniability." It's an old trick of the intelligence community to always provide a back door of plausible deniability whenever they dump secret information. And as it pertains to the whole Majestic 12 business, the phony Truman signature just might be the plausible deniability that they were banking on. Think about it. Some intelligence spook could drop off reams of paperwork divulging deep, dark secrets about UFOs and then paste a phony signature at the end of them. The contents are real, yet the signature is fake. The information gets out to the public, but the intelligence community has a way to plausibly deny the whole thing at the same time. That's the infamous backdoor out of full disclosure, used time and time again.

Another datum that makes a complete hoax seem unlikely is a Canadian government memo from 1950 in which a "defense project engineer" named Wilbur Smith states, "Flying saucers exist. Their modus operandi is unknown but concentrated effort is being made by a small group headed by Dr. Vannevar Bush." The fact that the Canadians knew that the U.S. had convened a study group on UFOs led by Dr. Vannevar Bush seems like confirmation of at least the existence of the Majestic 12.

So let's just forget about the seemingly bogus Truman signature for a moment and focus on the material itself. Much of the content pertains to the MJ-12 members and their backgrounds, and certain facts that were not known to the general public—such as Dr. Donald Menzel's "Top Secret Ultra" clearance—were apparently known by whoever produced the documents. It's also quite revealing that the documents were not released until shortly after the last living member of Majestic 12 had passed away.

According to the documents, in 1955 the U.S. military began a special program called Project Red Light whose objective was to reverse engineer recovered alien craft. This was the real purpose of Area 51 in the 1950s; yes, the U-2 was built and flown at this time, but it was essentially a sideshow. Area

51—itself code-named Dreamland—was also home to a second project called Snowbird, which was a misinformation campaign utilizing secret but man-made aircraft (such as the U-2) which to distract attention from the more exotic spacecraft that were being flown.

Were there two covert agendas at Area 51 at the same time? One in which conventional spy planes like the U-2 and the Blackbird were being built, and another even more secret operation in which alien spacecraft were being reverse engineered? The mystery is certainly intriguing, but as always, when push comes to shove, there is a way to plausibly deny just about all of it.

Sick Workers, Advanced Aerial Threats, and the Space Force

When most people think of Area 51, they either think of high-tech, top-secret U.S. military aircraft, or they ponder conspiracy theories about aliens and flying saucers. Very few, however, give much thought to the personnel who work at Area 51 every day. The fact is that Area 51 is a huge facility that requires thousands of staff to keep it running. From service members to civilian contractors, to specialists and technicians—there are an awful lot of people who get their paycheck from this secretive installation.

If you work at Area 51, your commute is a little bit different than it would be at most other employers. You can't just drive up and park in the parking garage. Instead, employees take a plane from the Las Vegas McCarran International Airport and fly in. And these planes are not your typical commercial airliners, either—they're JANET Airlines planes used only to fly folks in and out of Area 51. (The longstanding joke is that JANET stands for "Just Another Non-Existent Terminal," but the acronym actually stands for "Joint Air Network for Employee Transportation.")

Despite the drama, most of the people who board these planes are simply there to do a job. And most of these rank and file workers at Area 51 have no wild tales to tell about reverse-engineered alien spacecraft. Countless mechanics, janitors, nurses, and the like have worked at the facility for decades without reporting anything otherworldly taking place.

Of course, Bob Lazar claims that the whole base runs on a need to know basis, and that being the case, there is obviously no need for a cleaning crew mopping up an oil spill to know about the latest happenings on Zeta Reticuli. Nevertheless, everyone who flies into Area 51 must have a security clearance. According to Lazar, there are several levels of security clearances used in Area 51. The lowest level would be given to the most run of the mill security and maintenance staff. Higher levels would be handed out to those like Lazar who were actually made privy to alien technology. And even those who don't see anything important are bound not to discuss any detail of their work on the base.

That silence began to crack in the 1990s, however, when several former Area 51 technicians developed cancerous tumors due to the chemicals that they had been exposed to on site. Joe Bacco was one of them. He had done a lengthy sting at Area 51 during the 1970s, and he had been exposed to radiation from a number of nuclear tests. On one occasion, a nuclear blast had actually caused tremors severe enough to crack open several paved roads. It fell upon Bacco and his coworkers to repair the roads—and to receive horrible amounts of radiation while doing so. The radiation was intense enough to melt the asphalt they were using to repave the roads. It melted their gloves right off their hands. And as their ID badges melted off their uniforms, the mundane task of plugging up potholes became a truly hellish experience— one which would affect Joe Bacco for the rest of his life. His exposure to radiation that day severely damaged his skin, and ever afterward, the outer layer of his skin would blister and crack and he would sweat profusely.

Seeking compensation for his affliction, Bacco started legal proceedings against his former employer. His first problem with the case was that Area 51 officials had apparently deleted his personnel history; there was no record of him having worked at the base. His second was that the government was at that time still denying that the base even existed. It seemed like an airtight argument for Area 51's legal team: You can't sue us! You didn't work here, and we don't exist!

Bacco and his surviving coworkers didn't give up, though, and by the 1990s their case had gotten all the way to President Bill Clinton. The presiding judge, Philip Pro of the United States District Court for the District of Nevada, asked Clinton to declare any mention of the happenings at Area 51 a "threat to national security." And unfortunately for the wounded workers of Area 51, Clinton agreed. Due to the "presidential determination" that he signed, they could no longer be heard in court. Their attorney, George Washington University law professor Jonathan Turley (yes, the same Jonathan Turley who spoke in support of President Donald Trump during his impeachment) nevertheless continued to lobby ceaselessly for Area 51 to come clean.

However, it wouldn't be until 2013 that the facility rather abruptly announced what most of the world already knew— yes, we do exist. It was on August 16th of that year that the CIA finally admitted that Area 51 was a real and operational facility located somewhere in the Nevada desert. It's not entirely clear what prompted them to make this revelation at this particular point in time, but it's interesting to note that even as this acknowledgment was being made, the Pentagon was putting the brakes on a UFO investigation program that the public knew nothing about.

Knew nothing about, that is, until the *New York Times* decided to drop a bombshell news story about UFOs. Published on December 16, 2017, the article screamed out to the public with the bizarre headline of "Glowing Auras and 'Black Money': The Pentagon's Mysterious U.F.O. Program." Underneath, it highlighted a secret government program to investigate and identify UFOs, or as it called them, "Advanced Aerospace Threats."

The Advanced Aerospace Threat Identification Program (AATIP) ran from 2007 to 2012, and it apparently made some fairly startling findings. From what has been released so far, the U.S. military has had several well-documented encounters with craft that defied physics and did not appear to be anything the U.S. or any of its allies or adversaries were capable of producing.

One of these was the now-infamous Tic-Tac shaped UFO that fighter pilots encountered back in 2004. In startling video footage from the cockpit of a jet tasked with chasing the UFO, it can be seen tilting, rotating, and rapidly accelerating. Bob Lazar took one look at this footage and claimed that the craft behaved just like the ones he had seen at Area 51. He believes that the craft maneuvers by tilting on its side so that its onboard gravity amplifiers can use the force of gravity to send it shooting off in the opposite direction. The Pentagon was apparently quite interested in this craft, and massive research was conducted to investigate the sighting.

AATIP was officially axed in 2012, but in the summer of 2020 it came out that the program had merely changed its skin and continued under another name. Because right after the end of AATIP, the Pentagon fired up a basically identical research arm called the Unidentified Aerial Phenomena Task Force (UAPTF). Operating under the aegis of the U.S. Office of Naval Intelligence, this new UFO task force is apparently just a continuation of what began in 2007 with the AATIP.

Meanwhile, the U.S. military was expanding its own interstellar capabilities with the creation of the Space Force in 2019. This newest branch of the armed forces has provoked plenty of laughter on social media and late-night television; the name apparently conjures up images of goofy science fiction rather than military might. In fact, the Space Force is just following in the footsteps of the long-established Air Force, taking America's defensive to (literally) new heights. But that hasn't stopped the rumor mill in regard to the Space Force and its possible connections to Area 51 from going into overdrive. Is there some hidden reason why this new branch of the military was created so suddenly? Did the Advanced Aerospace Threat Identification Program identify something threatening? Only time will tell.

Should We Storm Area 51?

It started out as a joke. And as is the case with many jokes on the internet, it began with a kid running his mouth. American college student Matty Roberts was on Facebook one fine day when he had an epic daydream about what it would be like if millions of people flocked to Area 51 and stormed the gate. He captured this idea in a post entitled "Storm Area 51, They Can't Stop All of Us!" Under this heading, you could find the whimsical words of young Mr. Roberts stating, "We will all meet up at the Area 51 Alien Center tourist attraction and coordinate our entry. If we Naruto run, we can move faster than their bullets. Let's see them aliens!" (A "Naruto run" refers to an anime character named Naruto who runs in a particularly peculiar fashion.)

Although a joke, the post was created as a real Facebook event scheduled for September 20, 2019. The post went viral and over two million people selected the response "going" to indicate that they were planning to attend. They also began discussing everything from how they would break into Area 51, to exactly what they would do if they actually "saw them aliens." Some fantasized about freeing the aliens they presumed were being held prisoners. Others, disturbingly enough, talked about how they yearned to "clap alien cheeks." To put that in plain English, they wanted to have an encounter of the sexual kind with aliens. Yes, on the internet you can find all manner of people, saying all manner of shocking things, and in the summer of 2019, a good portion of them were flocking to Matty Roberts' crazy internet post.

Area 51 officials couldn't tell if what had indisputably started out as a joke had evolved into a serious security threat. But they wanted to be on the safe side, so they trotted out Air Force spokesperson Laura McAndrews to show that they meant business. As she stated, "[Area 51] is an open training range for the U.S. Air Force, and we would discourage anyone from trying to come into the area where we train American armed forces. The U.S. Air Force always stands ready to protect America and its assets."

As it turned out, the Air Force didn't have much to worry about. When it was all said and done, out of the two million who'd pledged to storm Area 51, only about 75 showed up at the gates. While there were a few arrests for trespassing, most of them just hung out and drank themselves into a stupor on the outskirts. So much for storming Area 51 to see "them aliens".

2020 saw a brief revival of the concept, with folks planning a reboot for the fall, but when the coronavirus pandemic took hold in the spring and hung on through the summer, it pretty much put the kibosh on any renewed attempts to storm Area 51.

The truth is, however, that if anywhere near two million people actually had swarmed the gates of Area 51, the Air Force would have been in a decidedly difficult position. As tough as they talked, there's no way that they would actually have started dropping bombs on civilians, or sent tanks careening through them. So, if two million true believers really did pop up at the gates of Area 51, would they really get to see them aliens? Don't bet on it.

Someday... We'll know the Truth

Area 51 is such a strange place. Perhaps that's the understatement of the century, but I just can't help but say it. It's strange on multiple levels. Area 51 seems to stand shoulder to shoulder in myth and legend with other mysterious locales such as Atlantis, Shangri-La, El Dorado, Neverland, and Oz—yet Area 51 itself is no myth. It's all too real. This is probably why the name Dreamland seems so apt a title for Area 51 because whenever anyone looks closely at its history, Area 51 does indeed seem like a place where dreams and reality merge.

This is due to the dual nature of our knowledge about this most infamous facility. You see, even though we know and it's been officially confirmed that Area 51 exists, we still have no clue as to what really goes on there. Even if it's just top-secret military projects with conventional human-based technology, us normal civilians are not considered worthy enough to know the inner workings of the base. And without any clear knowledge of what might be taking place, the mind is going to do a bit of wandering.

But the immense number of conspiracy theories and conjectures regarding Area 51 cannot simply be written off as idle speculation about the happenings on a top-secret military base. There are, after all, many military installations all over the world in which the average civilian is not allowed to set foot. Every nation has military projects that it does not wish prying eyes to see. Yet there is something about Area

51 that has captured the public's imagination like nothing else.

Too many people have reported unworldly things emanating from this one piece of ground, for it to be dismissed as imaginations run wild. If someone like Bob Lazar suddenly confessed to pulling a major hoax, perhaps it would take some of the wind out of the conspiratorial sails. But Lazar and countless others have stuck to their stories.

About the only item related to Area 51 conspiracy theories that has been called into serious question is the supposed Majestic 12 material, which some claim contains a copy-pasted signature of President Harry S. Truman. Yet even if this signature is fake, several other facets of the MJ-12 documents seem to bolster and corroborate several other Area 51 claims.

In military intelligence, there is something called "plausible deniability" in which real data is leaked with just enough disinformation that it can be denied later on. Some believe the Majestic 12 documents serve this purpose. According to this theory, someone, somewhere, wanted to get real intelligence about Area 51 and other UFO data out there, yet they put a copied signature on the documents so that they could be denied later on.

For those obsessed with the mythos that revolves around this very real military installation, the search for answers can be frustrating. It almost makes them want to take matters into their own hands—or at least two million internet users' hands—and storm the base. But as the Storm Area 51 fad of 2019 proved, such things are fun to joke about but unworkable in practice. No, we won't get the answers we are looking for by storming Area 51. We aren't going to force these secrets to be revealed to us. But nevertheless, one day soon, maybe we'll know the truth.

Further Readings

Now that we've brought this book to a close, let's take a look at some of the reading and reference materials that helped to make it all possible. Here you will find a wide variety of perspectives on many of the topics discussed. Feel free to look them up for yourself.

Dreamland: Travels Inside the Secret World of Roswell and Area 51. Phil Patton

This book details the roads less traveled at Area 51. Phil Patton talks to those that have either worked at the base or have tried really hard to get inside. Of particular interest, was his discussion of former workers at the base who became ill and later sued the U.S. government for compensation.

Keep Out! Top Secret Places Governments Don't Want You to Know About. Nick Redfern

Nick Redfern has written quite a few books about the mysterious and the unknown. It only makes sense that he would write up a piece on Area 51. This book showcases not just the Nevada base but several other mysterious locales. It's an informative as well as an entertaining read.

Beyond Area 51: The mysteries of the planet's most forbidden, top secret destinations. Mack Maloney

Mr. Maloney takes a look at some of the strangest conspiracy theories you've ever (or never) heard about Area 51. This book was useful in gleaning details about some of the more obscure pieces of testimony in regard to Area 51. This book also has quite useful information about Bob Lazar.

Dreamland: An Autobiography. Bob Lazar

This book is highly informative. Bob Lazar's story hasn't changed much throughout the years. In this autobiographical telling, however, he does share some rather intriguing perspective and background information never shared before.

Printed in Great Britain
by Amazon